Progettare e disegnare stampe per tessuti

Как конструировать и рисовать_____нты

Cómo crear y d_____da

Design und Zeichnungen von Fashion Prints

Création et dessin d'imprimés mode

ELISABETTA 'KUKY' DRUDI

THE PEPIN PRESS
AMSTERDAM • SINGAPORE

The Pepin Press
P.O. Box 10349
1001 EH Amsterdam
T +31 20 4202021
F +31 20 4201152
mail@pepinpress.com
www.pepinpress.com

Concept & Drawings: Elisabetta 'Kuky' Drudi
Text: Elisabetta 'Kuky' Drudi with additions by Kevin Haworth
Project management: Kevin Haworth
Editorial supervision & Design: Pepin van Roojen
Layout: Margreet Mulder, Kevin Haworth & Pepin van Roojen
Copy-editing: Cambridge Editorial Partnership

ISBN 978 90 5496 140 6

2014 13 12 11 10 09 08
10 9 8 7 6 5 4 3 2 1

Printed in Singapore

Elisabetta 'Kuky' Drudi obtained her degree at the Istituto d'Arte
F. Mengaroni in Pesaro, Italy. Since then, she has worked as a designer
and illustrator for many well-known international fashion houses. She has
written *Figure Drawing for Fashion Design* (together with Tiziana Paci),
Wrap & Drape Fashion and *Fabric: Textures & Patterns*, all published by
The Pepin Press in several languages.
Elisabetta Drudi continues to be very active, creating fashion and textile
designs for world famous brands.

Thanks to:
Stefano, my boyfriend, for his constructive suggestions and brilliant
supervision;
the painter Jana Cavallari Drudi, my mother, for her help with historical and
stylistic research;
my brother Mauro, writer, for his linguistic supervision;
the stylist Karen McCausland, who encouraged me to make this book.

Contents | Contenuti | Inhalt | Contenu | Содержание | Contenido

Free CD-ROM inside the back cover

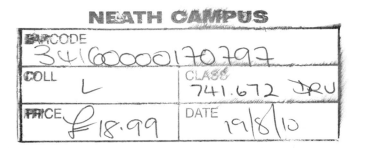

English

There are many ways to go about designing a fashion print. In this book, we have illustrated a selection of techniques that can be applied in almost limitless combinations.

This first chapter contains step-by-step instructions and examples on how to work with simple and complex elements, combine elements to create patterns, use layers and colours, and make quick spin-off patterns.

The remaining chapters illustrate these techniques and provide examples of fashion prints. Each chapter makes use of a unique style and colour palette.

Italiano

Ci sono molti modi per disegnare un tessuto stampato. In questo libro illustrato viene mostrata una selezione di tecniche che possono essere applicate in combinazioni quasi illimitate.

Il primo capitolo contiene le istruzioni passo a passo e gli esempi di come lavorare con elementi semplici e complessi, di come combinare i vari elementi per creare disegni, utilizzare livelli e colori e sviluppare in poco tempo nuovi schemi a partire da quelli appena preparati.

I capitoli successivi illustrano queste tecniche e forniscono esempi di tessuti stampati. Ogni capitolo rappresenta un unico stile e un'unica gamma di colori.

Deutsch

»Fashion Prints« (Mode- oder Textildrucke) lassen sich auf viele unterschiedliche Arten entwerfen - und in diesem Buch finden Sie eine große Auswahl von Designtechniken, die sich nahezu unbegrenzt miteinander kombinieren lassen.

Das erste Kapitel erklärt Schritt für Schritt und anhand von Beispielen, wie man mit schlichten und komplexen Elementen arbeitet, wie sich einzelne Elemente zu neuen Mustern kombinieren lassen, wie man Schichten und Farben verwendet und wie sich aus bekannten Designs schnell neue Muster (so genannte »Spin-off Prints«) machen lassen.

In den übrigen Kapiteln werden diese Techniken auch bildlich beschrieben und mit Beispielen bekannter Modedrucke illustriert. Dabei greift jedes Kapitel auf eine eigenständige Stil- und Farbpalette zurück.

Français

Il existe de nombreuses manières de créer des imprimés mode. Vous trouverez ici une sélection de techniques illustrées et réalisables dans des combinaisons pratiquement illimitées.

Ce premier chapitre contient des instructions pas-à-pas ainsi que des exemples de réalisation d'éléments simples et complexes, de combinaisons d'éléments pour créer des motifs, d'utilisation de couches et de couleurs et d'élaboration rapide de motifs reproduits.

Les autres chapitres illustrent ces techniques et présentent des exemples d'imprimés mode. Chaque chapitre s'appuie sur une palette de couleurs et de styles propre.

Русский

Существует множество способов создания стилевых орнаментов. В этой книге мы проиллюстрировали ряд методов, которые можно применять в практически бесконечном количестве комбинаций.

В первой главе даны пошаговые инструкции и описаны примеры работы с простыми и сложными элементами, с сочетаниями элементов для создания орнаментов, проиллюстрировано использование слоев и цветов, а также описан процесс быстрого выделения орнаментов.

В остальных главах эти методы проиллюстрированы и даны примеры стилевых орнаментов. В каждой из глав используется свой уникальный стиль и своя цветовая палитра.

Español

Existen multitud de modos de acometer el diseño de un estampado de moda. En este libro se recoge una selección de técnicas que pueden aplicarse en combinaciones prácticamente ilimitadas.

El primer capítulo contiene instrucciones paso a paso y ejemplos para trabajar con elementos simples y complejos, combinarlos para crear diseños, aplicar capas y colores, y derivar rápidamente estampados nuevos de otros ya existentes.

En los capítulos restantes se ilustran estas técnicas y se reproducen muestras de estampados de tejidos. Cada capítulo está dedicado a una paleta de color y a un estilo únicos.

Chapter
Capitolo
Kapitel
Chapitre
Глава
Capítulo

1

Design elements

Each chapter begins with a collection of design elements that set its style and colour palette. Design elements for Chapter 1 are shown on pages 9 and 10.

Page 11 shows several techniques that can be used with design elements to create new composite elements or to form simple patterns.

Over 1000 geometric and floral design elements are provided in this book so that you can create fashion prints in a variety of styles. All of these elements are included on the accompanying CD.

Elementi di design

Ogni capitolo inizia con una serie di elementi di design che ne segnano lo stile e la gamma di colori. Gli elementi di design del capitolo 1 sono mostrati a pagina 9 e 10.

A pagina 11 si vedono varie tecniche che possono essere impiegate per creare nuovi elementi composti o per formare schemi semplici.

Questo libro fornisce oltre 1000 fantasie floreali e geometriche, contenute nel CD accluso, grazie alle quali potrete creare tessuti stampati personalizzati, in una grande varietà di stili.

Design-Elemente

Jedes Kapitel beginnt mit einer Kollektion von Designelementen, welche die jeweilige Stil- und Farbpalette definieren. Die im Kapitel 1 verwendeten Designelemente finden Sie beispielsweise auf den Seiten 9 und 10.

Seite 11 präsentiert verschiedene Techniken, mit denen sich aus den vorgestellten Designelementen neue Elemente zusammenstellen oder einfache Muster kreieren lassen.

Dieses Buch enthält über 1.000 geometrische und florale Designelemente, aus denen sich eine unendliche Zahl neuer, kreativer »Fashion Prints« ergibt. Selbstverständlich sind alle im Buch vorgestellten Designmuster auch auf der beiliegenden CD-ROM enthalten.

Éléments de style

Au début de chaque chapitre se trouve une collection d'éléments de style présentant sa palette de couleurs et de styles. Les éléments de style du chapitre 1 se trouvent aux pages 9 et 10.

La page 11 présente diverses techniques utilisables avec des éléments de style pour créer des éléments composites ou pour former des motifs simples.

Plus de 1 000 éléments de style géométriques et floraux sont proposés dans ce livre pour créer des imprimés mode dans des styles variés. Tous ces éléments se trouvent également sur le disque fourni.

Элементы дизайна

Каждая из глав начинается с коллекции элементов дизайна, составляющих стиль и цветовую палитру. Элементы дизайна для Главы 1 показаны на страницах 9 и 10.

На странице 11 продемонстрировано несколько методик, которые можно использовать в работе с элементами дизайна для создания новых составных элементов или образования простых орнаментов.

В этой книге представлено свыше 1000 геометрических и цветочных элементов дизайна, так что вы можете создавать орнаменты в самых разнообразных стилях. Все эти элементы содержатся на прилагаемом компакт-диске.

Elementos de diseño

Cada capítulo abre con una colección de elementos de diseño que define el estilo y la paleta de color empleados. Los elementos de diseño del capítulo 1 se muestran en las páginas 9 y 10.

La página 11 presenta varias técnicas con las que crear elementos compuestos o estampados simples a partir de elementos de diseño sencillos.

En estas páginas se recogen más de mil elementos de diseño geométricos y florales con los cuales podrá crear estampados de moda de los más diversos estilos. Todos estos elementos se incluyen también en el CD adjunto.

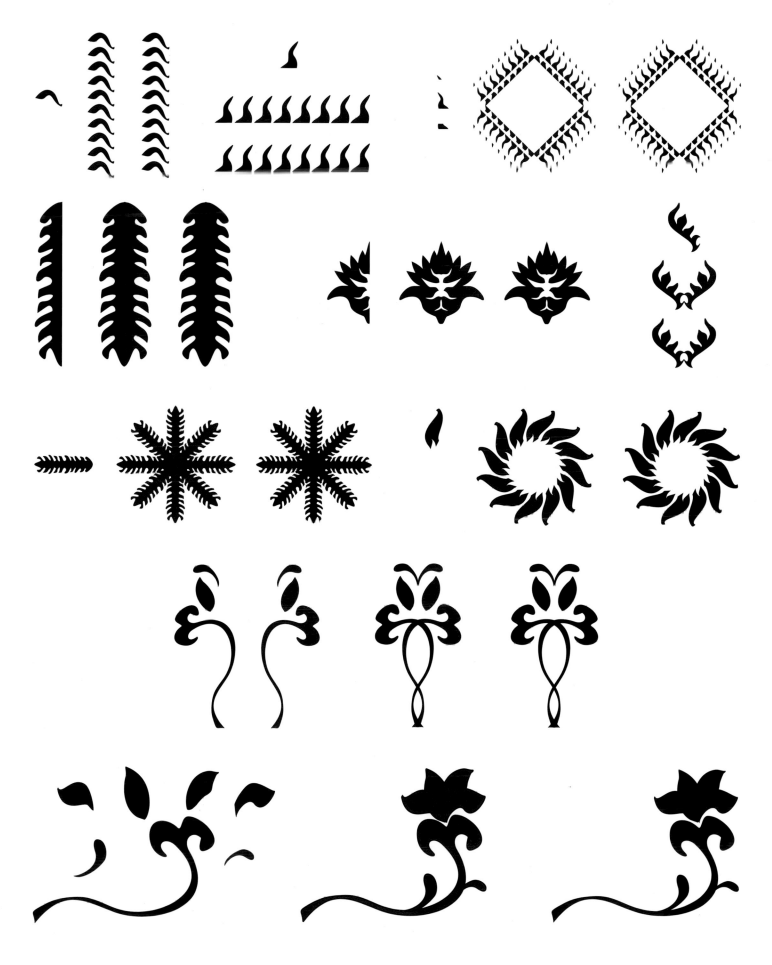

Simple Fashion Prints

The simplest method of making a print is to work with just one design element. Each of the six patterns shown on the following page was made in this way. Each single element has endless possibilities.

Tessuti stampati semplici

Il modo più semplice per creare uno schema di stampa è quello di lavorare con un solo elemento della stampa. Ciascuno degli schemi mostrati nella prossima pagina è stato creato in questo modo. Ogni singolo elemento ha infinite possibilità di sviluppo.

Einfache Modedrucke

Am einfachsten lässt sich ein Druck mit nur einem einzigen Designelement erstellen - und jedes der sechs Muster, die auf der folgenden Seite gezeigt werden, ist auf diese Weise entstanden. Sie sehen also: Selbst ein einzelnes Designelement birgt bereits endlose Möglichkeiten in sich.

Imprimés mode simples

La méthode la plus simple pour réaliser un imprimé consiste à travailler avec un seul élément de style. Les six éléments de la page suivante ont été élaborés de cette manière. Chaque élément présente une infinité de possibilités.

Простые стилевые орнаменты

Самый простой метод создания орнамента состоит в том, чтобы работать со всего одним элементом дизайна. Каждый из шести показанных на следующей странице орнаментов был получен именно таким образом. Каждый из одиночных элементов предоставляет бесчисленное множество возможностей.

Estampados de moda simples

El método más sencillo para crear un estampado consiste en trabajar con un único elemento de diseño. Los seis estampados que se muestran en la página siguiente se elaboraron de este modo. Cada elemento por sí solo ofrece infinitud de posibilidades.

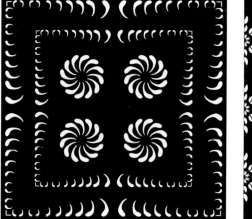

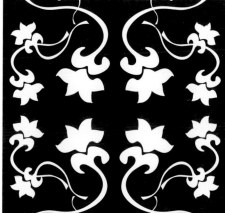

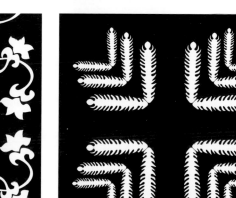

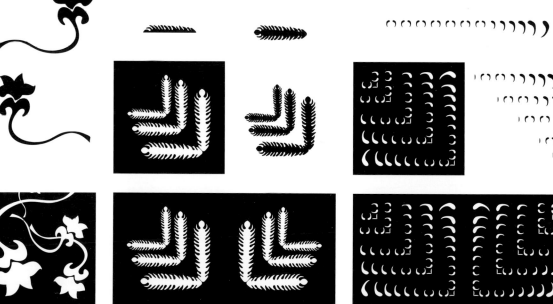

Using a Design Block

More complex patterns can be made by creating a basic design block and repeating and/or mirroring it to form a larger pattern. Page 15 shows how a range of shapes can be combined and reproduced. For Chapter 1, we used a triangular design block made from elements found on pages 10 and 11.

Page 16 shows three approaches to reproducing this triangle (**A**, **B** and **C**). Note that all three give the same final result. Shifting the centre point of rotation and/or mirroring produces a different result (**D**).

This fourth print (**D**) is smaller than the first three because it has only been repeated four times. If a larger print is desired, this square print can easily be repeated to make a larger one (**E**).

Lavorare con un disegno-base

Si possono disegnare campioni più complessi creando un disegno base semplice e ripetendolo e/o riflettendolo fino a formare uno schema più grande. A pagina 15 si vede come una serie di forme può essere combinata e riprodotta. Per il capitolo 1 abbiamo usato un disegno-base triangolare, creato a partire dagli elementi di pagina 10 e 11.

A pagina 16 si possono vedere tre modi per riprodurre questo triangolo (**A**, **B** e **C**). È importante rilevare che alla fine si ottiene sempre lo stesso risultato.Spostando il punto centrale della rotazione e/o della forma con la parte riflessa si ottiene un risultato diverso (**D**).

Questo quarto disegno (**D**) è più piccolo degli altri tre perché il disegno-base è stato ripetuto solo quattro volte. Se si desidera un disegno finale più grande, basterà ripetere questo primo risultato e se ne otterrà uno di dimensioni maggiori (**E**).

Arbeit mit einem Musterblock

Etwas komplexere Designs entstehen, wenn man einen einfachen Musterblock mehrfach nutzt und so ein größeres Muster anlegt. Seite 15 zeigt, wie sich auf diese Weise eine große Auswahl von Formen kombinieren und reproduzieren lässt. So wurde in Kapitel 1 ein dreieckiger Musterblock benutzt, der aus Elementen besteht, die auf den Seiten 10 und 11 zu sehen sind.

Auf Seite 16 finden Sie drei Möglichkeiten zur Reproduktion dieses Dreiecks (**A**, **B** und **C**) - wobei alle drei Wege interessanterweise zum gleichen Endresultat führen. Durch eine Verschiebung des Rotationsmittelpunkts und/ oder eine Spiegelung erzielt man dagegen ein ganz anderes Ergebnis (**D**).

Dieser vierte Modedruck (**D**) ist kleiner als die ersten drei Beispiele, da das Muster nur vier Mal wiederholt wurde. Sollten Sie einen größeren Druck erzielen wollen, lässt sich das durch eine Wiederholung dieses quadratischen Musters erreichen (**E**).

Utilisation d'un bloc de style

Il est possible de créer des motifs plus complexes en partant d'un bloc de style de base, répété et/ou réfléchi de façon à former un motif plus étendu. La page 15 montre comment assembler et reproduire une gamme de formes. Le chapitre 1 s'appuie sur un bloc de style triangulaire réalisé à partir d'éléments des pages 10 et 11.

La page 16 propose trois manières de reproduire ce triangle (**A**, **B** et **C**). Ces trois approches offrent le même résultat. Le déplacement du point de rotation ou de l'axe de l'effet miroir produit cependant un résultat différent (**D**).

Ce quatrième imprimé (**D**) est plus petit que les trois premiers car il est répété quatre fois seulement. Si vous désirez obtenir un motif plus grand, cet imprimé peut facilement être répété pour en réaliser un plus grand (**E**).

Использование блока дизайна

Более сложные орнаменты можно составлять, создавая базовый блок дизайна и повторяя и/или зеркально отображая его так, чтобы образовать более крупный орнамент. На странице 15 показано, как можно сочетать и воспроизводить ряд форм. В Главе 1 мы используем треугольный блок дизайна, составленный из элементов, найденных на страницах 10 и 11.

На странице 16 проиллюстрированы три подхода к воспроизведению этого треугольника (**A**, **B** и **C**). Обратите внимание, что применение всех трех подходов дает один и тот же окончательный результат. Смещение и/или зеркальное отображение точки центра вращения приводит к получению иного результата (**D**).

Четвертый орнамент (**D**) меньше первых трех, поскольку он повторен лишь четыре раза. Если необходим более крупный орнамент, этот квадратный орнамент легко повторить для получения более крупного (**E**).

Diseñar con bloques

Para crear estampados más complejos conviene componer un bloque de diseño básico y repetirlo y/o reflejarlo formando un dibujo de mayores proporciones. En la página 15 se ilustra cómo combinar y reproducir una variedad de formas. En el capítulo 1 se utilizó un bloque de diseño triangular integrado por elementos de las páginas 10 y 11.

La página 16 recoge tres formas distintas de reproducir el mismo triángulo (**A**, **B** y **C**). Todas ellas generan el mismo resultado final. En cambio, si se modifica el punto central de rotación y/o el reflejo, se obtiene un estampado distinto (**D**).

Este cuarto estampado (**D**) es de menores dimensiones que los otros tres porque solo se ha repetido cuatro veces. Para crear un estampado más grande (**E**) basta con repetir este retazo cuadrado.

A   B   C

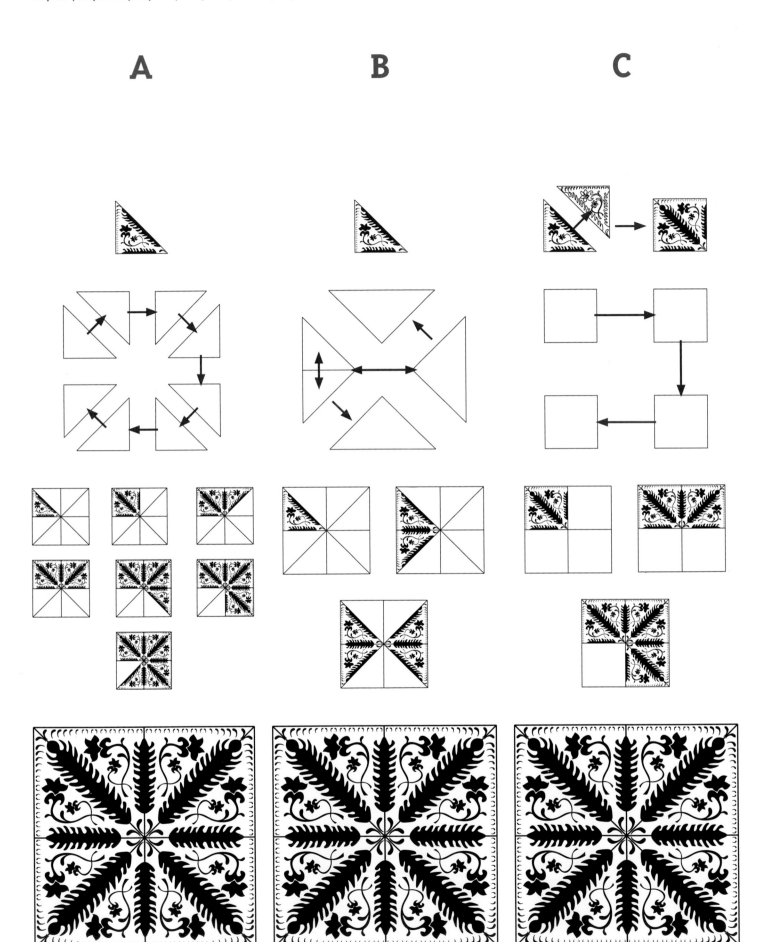

Point of rotation

Punto di rotazione

Rotationspunkt

Point de rotation

Точки вращения

Punto de rotación

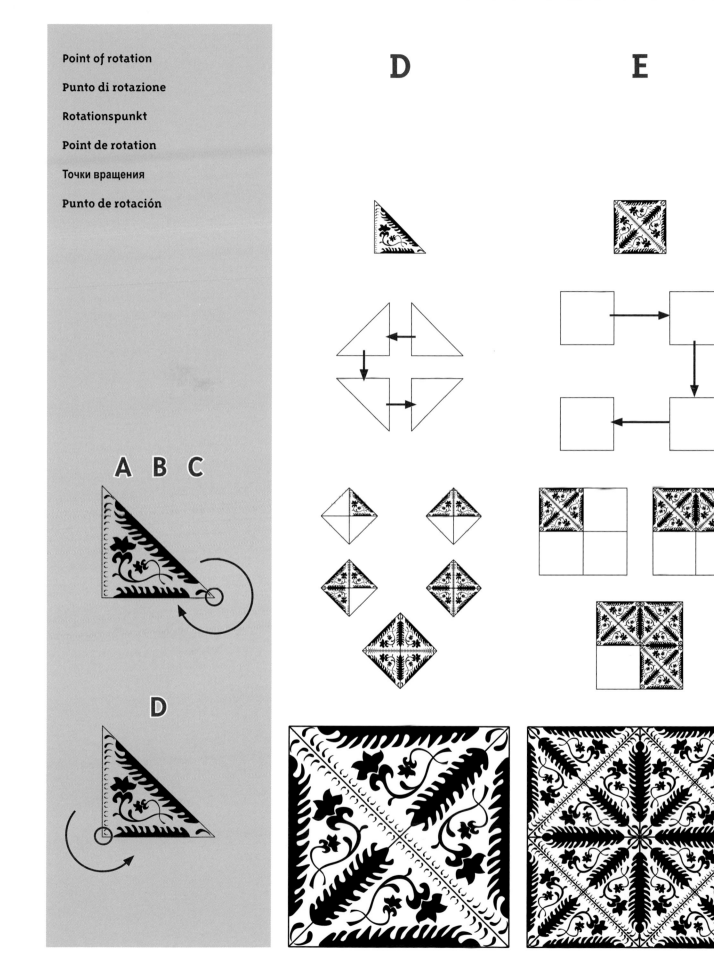

A B C

D

D

E

Layers and Colours

The appearance of the final print can be changed significantly by introducing a background colour or pattern. A background pattern can be made using the method shown on pages 16 and 17.

Once a pattern has been achieved, a negative version can be produced by inverting the colours. Both the positive (*P*) and negative (*N*) versions are useful in designing fashion prints.

The use of this background and the pattern from page 16 results in four different fashion prints. Any number of variations can be made simply by changing the colours, layering and transparency of these two patterns.

Livelli e colori

L'aspetto del disegno finale può essere cambiato in maniera significativa introducendo un colore o uno schema che facciano da sfondo. Si può creare uno schema per lo sfondo utilizzando il metodo mostrato alle pagine 16 e 17.

Una volta ottenuto lo schema, se ne può produrre una versione in negativo invertendo i colori. Entrambe le versioni, quella positiva (*P*) e quella negativa (*N*) sono utili nella creazione di tessuti stampati.

L'uso di questo sfondo e degli schemi di pagina 16 danno quattro diversi tessuti stampati. Variando semplicemente i colori, i livelli e la trasparenza di questi due disegni si può ottenere un'ampia serie di variazioni.

Schichten und Farben

Das endgültige Erscheinungsbild eines Modedrucks lässt sich durch die Nutzung einer Hintergrundfarbe oder eines Hintergrundmusters stark verändern. Wie man derartige Hintergrundmuster anlegt, wird auf den Seiten 16 und 17 gezeigt.

Sobald ein Muster angelegt ist, lässt sich durch die Umkehrung der Farben eine »Negativ-Version« erzielen - und sowohl den Positivdruck (*P*) als auch den Negativdruck (*N*) kann man beim Entwurf von Fashion Prints sinnvoll und kreativ einsetzen.

So entstanden z.B. aus dem auf Seite 16 vorgestellten Muster und Hintergrund vier verschiedene Modedrucke. Durch einfaches Austauschen der Farben sowie durch Umschichtung oder Transparenz dieser beiden Muster lassen sich eine Vielzahl von Variationen kreieren.

Couches et couleurs

Vous pouvez modifier nettement l'apparence du résultat en introduisant un motif ou une couleur de fond. Pour ce faire, suivez la méthode indiquée aux pages 16 et 17.

Après avoir achevé un motif, il est possible de reproduire une version négative en inversant les couleurs. La version positive (*P*) et la version négative (*N*) sont toutes deux utiles à la création d'imprimés mode.

Ce fond combiné au motif de la page 16 produit quatre imprimés mode différents. Des variantes peuvent être obtenues en changeant simplement la couleur, la couche et la transparence de ces deux motifs.

Слои и цвета

Внешний вид готового орнамента легко существенно изменить, введя фоновый цвет или узор. Фоновый узор можно составить, используя метод, проиллюстрированный на страницах 16 and 17.

Разработав орнамент, можно создать его негативную версию, выполнив обращение цветов. При конструировании стилевых орнаментов полезны как позитивная (*P*), так и негативная (*N*) версии.

Использование этого фона и орнамента со страницы 16 приводит к получению четырех различных стилевых орнаментов. Простым изменением цветов, слоев и степени прозрачности этих двух орнаментов можно составить любое количество вариантов.

Capas y colores

El aspecto del estampado final puede modificarse de forma significativa aplicando un color o una trama de fondo. Para crear una trama de fondo puede emplearse el método ilustrado en las páginas 16 y 17.

Una vez conseguido un diseño, es posible generar su versión negativa invirtiendo los colores. Tanto la variante positiva (*P*) como la negativa (*N*) resultan útiles para diseñar estampados de moda.

La combinación de este fondo con el diseño de la página 16 permite crear cuatro estampados distintos. Pueden obtenerse infinidad de variantes mediante la simple modificación de los colores y la aplicación de capas y transparencias a estos dos diseños.

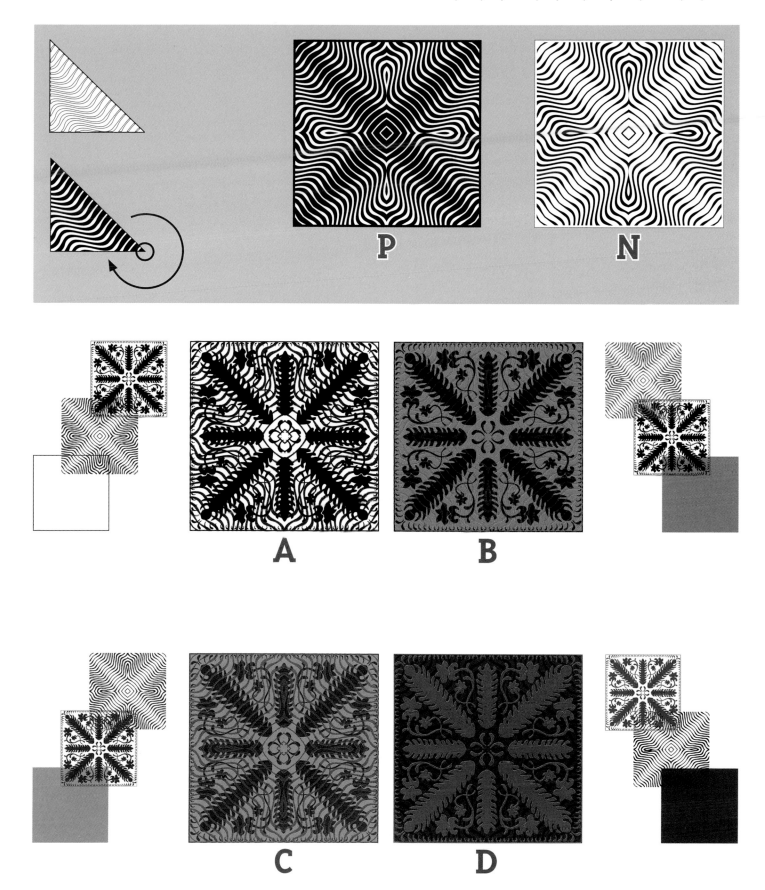

Spin-off Prints

Even after a print is complete, the design process can continue. Pieces of any existing design can be used to create entirely new prints.

On pages 21 and 22, sections have been extracted from the four existing prints to make new spin-offs. As you can see, these selections can be extracted in any shape or size. The system for reproducing these shapes is limited only by the designer's imagination.

This process of making spin-offs can be taken a step further. On page 23, four selections from a pattern (*a*, *b*, *c* and *d*) are extracted and repeated. The resulting (mini) patterns are then combined (*e*) and a new design block (*f*) is used to develop an entirely new print.

Nuovi schemi derivati dai precedenti

Una volta che lo schema è pronto, si può portare avanti il processo di creazione. Le parti di uno schema già esistente possono essere usate per creare dei disegni completamente nuovi.

A pagina 21 e 22 vengono mostrate alcune sezioni dei quattro schemi già esistenti, e se ne sono creati di nuovi. Come si evince dalle immagini, le sezioni possono essere di qualsiasi forma o dimensione. L'unico limite è l'immaginazione del designer.

Il processo di creazione di schemi derivati può spingersi ancora oltre. A pagina 23 si sono scelte quattro sezioni di uno schema (*a*, *b*, *c* e *d*) e si sono ripetute. I (mini) campioni che ne sono risultati sono stati poi combinati (*e*) e il risultato (*f*) è stato impiegato come disegno-base per una nuova stampa.

Spin-off Prints

Auch nach der Kreation eines Modedrucks kann dessen Designprozess noch fortgeführt werden; schließlich lassen sich aus Teilen bereits existierender Designs völlig neue Muster erstellen - die so genannten »Spin-off Prints«.

Auf den Seiten 21 und 22 wurden Teile der bereits existierenden vier Modedrucke zu neuen »Ablegern« kombiniert - und wie Sie sehen können, lassen sich diese Ausschnitte in Form und Größe beliebig ausdehnen. Die Reproduktion solcher Formen wird letztlich nur durch die Phantasie ihrer Designer begrenzt.

Die Erstellung derartiger »Spin-offs« lässt sich sogar noch einen Schritt weiter führen: So wurden auf Seite 23 vier Ausschnitte eines Musters (*a*, *b*, *c* und *d*) neu kombiniert und wiederholt und die daraus hervorgegangenen (kleinen) Muster ebenfalls neu zusammengestellt (*e*), so dass ein neuer Musterblock (*f*) entstand, mit dem sich wiederum völlig neue Designs kreieren lassen.

Reproductions d'imprimés

Le processus de création peut continuer même après qu'un imprimé est terminé. Des parties d'un style peuvent être réutilisées pour créer des imprimés entièrement nouveaux.

Sur les pages 21 et 22, des parties ont été extraites des quatre imprimés existants pour réaliser des reproductions dérivées. Comme vous le voyez, ces sélections peuvent présenter n'importe quelle forme ou taille. Le système de reproduction des formes est uniquement limité par l'imagination du créateur.

Le procédé de réalisation de ces reproductions dérivées peut aller plus loin. La page 23 présente quatre sélections d'un motif (*a*, *b*, *c* et *d*) extraites puis répétées. Les (mini) motifs produits sont ensuite assemblés (*e*) en un nouveau bloc de style (*f*) servant à développer un imprimé entièrement nouveau.

Выделенные орнаменты

Даже после того, как создание орнамента завершается, процесс конструирования может продолжаться. Детали любого существующего дизайна можно использовать для разработки совершенно новых орнаментов.

На страницах 21 и 22 проиллюстрировано извлечение деталей из четырех существующих орнаментов для создания новых выделенных орнаментов. Как показано на иллюстрации, можно «извлекать» детали любой формы и размеров. Способы воспроизведения этих форм не имеют никаких ограничений, кроме воображения дизайнера.

Этот процесс «почкования» можно распространить еще на шаг вперед. На странице 23 извлечены и повторены четыре детали орнамента (*a*, *b*, *c* и *d*). Полученные (мини)орнаменты затем скомбинированы (*e*), и новый блок дизайна (*f*) используется для разработки совершенно нового орнамента.

Estampados derivados

La obtención de un estampado definitivo no conlleva necesariamente el fin del proceso de diseño. A partir de fragmentos del estampado existente pueden generarse otros completamente nuevos.

En las páginas 21 y 22 se han extraído retazos de los cuatro estampados existentes para componer nuevos derivados. Como puede ver, estos fragmentos presentan formas y tamaños diversos. El único límite para crear nuevos diseños es la imaginación del diseñador.

El proceso de creación de estampados derivados puede llevarse aún más lejos. En la página 23 se han extraído y repetido cuatro fragmentos de un diseño (*a*, *b*, *c* y *d*). Los (mini) estampados resultantes se han combinado (*e*) y se ha generado un bloque de diseño nuevo (*f*) para obtener un estampado muy diferente.

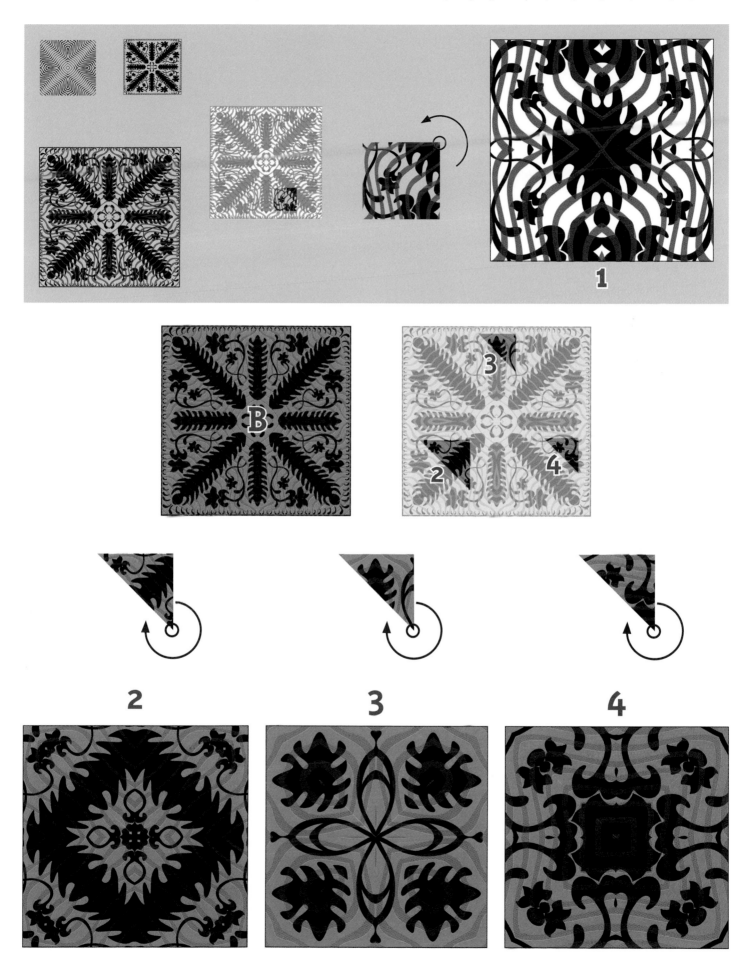

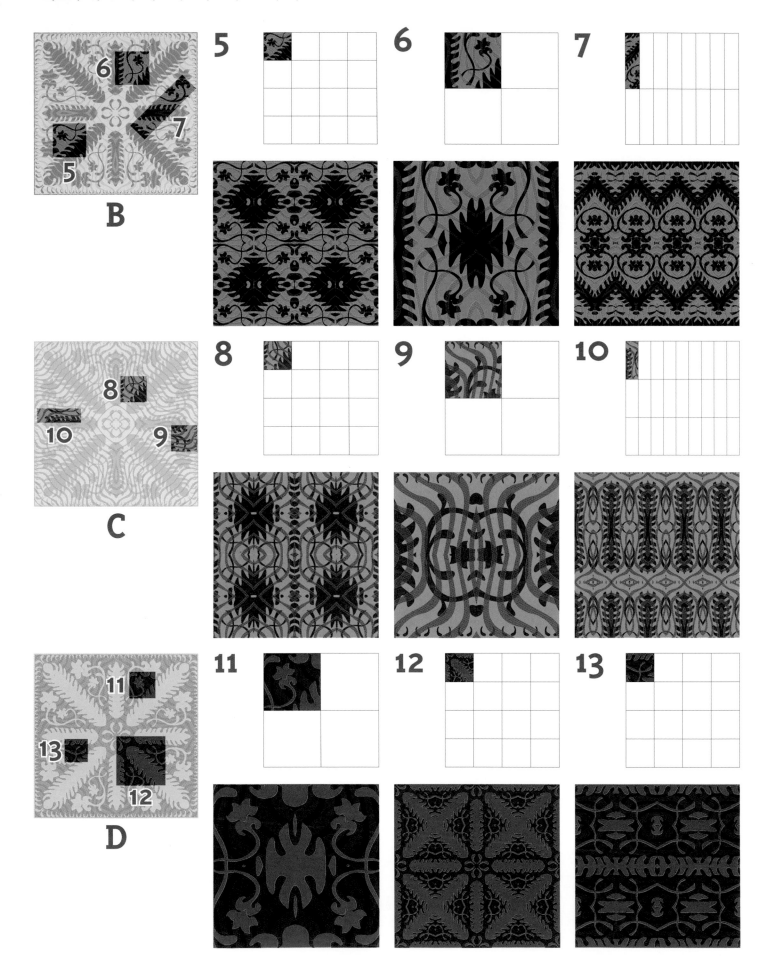

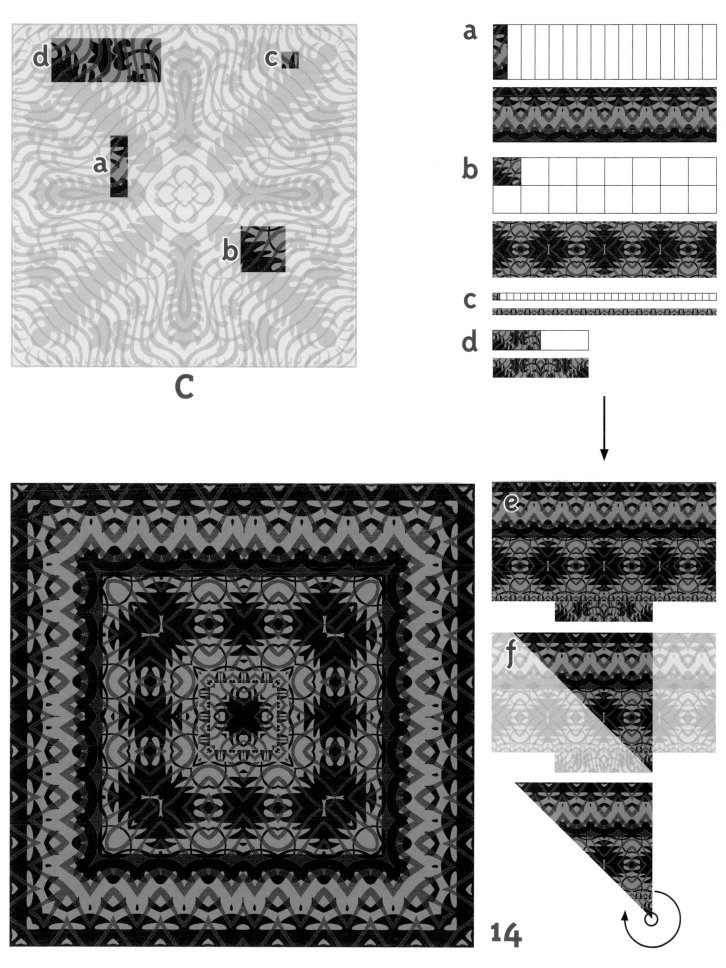

C

14

Fashion Plates

The methods described in this book can be used to create fashion prints for any purpose, but are ideally suited to designing one-piece garments such as wraps, shawls, scarves and sarongs. Each chapter includes a number of drawings illustrating how to draw a model and incorporate clothing and prints to create a fashion plate.

For more detailed instructions on drawing fashion plates and designing draped fashion, we recommend two other titles in this Pepin Press series: *Figure Drawing for Fashion Design*, written by Elisabetta Drudi and Tiziana Paci, and *Wrap and Drape Fashion*, written by Elisabetta Drudi. Both of these books are excellent companions to *Fashion Prints*.

Figurini

I metodi descritti in questo libro possono essere impiegati per creare tessuti stampati per ogni impiego, ma sono ideali per disegnare indumenti di un solo pezzo come scialli, sciarpe e sarong. Ogni capitolo comprende un numero di immagini che illustrano come disegnare un modello e incorporare gli indumenti e i motivi per creare un figurino.

Per istruzioni più dettagliate sui figurini e su come disegnare indumenti come quelli descritti si consiglia la lettura di altri due libri di questa stessa serie della casa editrice Pepin Press: *Figure Drawing for Fashion Design* scritto da Elisabetta Drudi e Tiziana Paci, e *Wrap and Drape Fashion: Moda da avvolgere e drappeggiare* scritto da Elisabetta Drudi. Entrambi i libri sono il complemento ideale di *Fashion Prints*.

Modezeichnungen

Mit den in diesem Buch beschriebenen Methoden lassen sich Modedrucke für jeden Zweck erstellen, vor allem aber für den Entwurf einteiliger Textilien wie Pareos, Schals, Halstücher oder Sarongs. In jedem Kapitel wird anhand von Skizzen erläutert, wie man Mode-Figurinen und Kleidungsstücke zeichnet und mit Hilfe von Musterdrucken eine Modezeichnung erstellt.

Für genauere Informationen über die Gestaltung von Modezeichnungen und den Entwurf von einteiliger Mode empfehlen wir Ihnen zwei weitere Bücher aus dieser Pepin Press-Reihe: *Zeichnen für Modedesign* (von Elisabetta Drudi und Tiziana Paci) und *Wrap and Drape Fashion: Einteilige Mode - Geschichte, Entwurf & Zeichnung* (von Elisabetta Drudi). Beide Bände eignen sich ideal als Ergänzung zu *Fashion Prints*.

Planches mode

Les méthodes décrites tout au long de ce livre permettent de créer des imprimés mode pour tous usages mais elles conviennent principalement à la création de vêtements une pièce, tels que les châles, les écharpes et les sarongs. Tous les chapitres comprennent un certain nombre de dessins expliquant comment tracer un modèle et fusionner le tissu et les imprimés pour créer une planche mode.

Pour des instructions plus amples sur le dessin des planches mode et la création de vêtements drapés, nous vous recommandons deux autres titres de la série Pepin Press : *Figurines de mode et stylisme*, écrit par Elisabetta Drudi et Tiziana Paci, et *La mode du drapé*, par Elisabetta Drudi. Ces deux livres qui s'avèrent d'excellents compléments à *Fashion Prints*.

Стилевые пластины

Методы, описанные в этой книге, можно использовать для разработки стилевых орнаментов любого назначения, но в первую очередь они идеально подходят для разработки деталей одежды, таких как платки, шали, шарфы, галстуки и саронги. Каждая из глав содержит множество рисунков, иллюстрирующих процесс рисования модели, соединения одежды и орнаментов с целью создания стилевой пластины.

За более подробными инструкциями по разработке стилевых пластин и конструированию моделей мы рекомендуем обратиться к двум другим изданиям Pepin Press: *Рисование фигур для моделей одежды* (Figure Drawing for Fashion Design), написанной Элизабетой Друди (Elisabetta Drudi) и Татьяной Паци (Tiziana Paci), и *Стили драпирования* (Wrap and Drape Fashion), написанной Элизабетой Друди. Обе эти книги прекрасно сочетаются с книгой *Fashion Prints*.

Ilustraciones de moda

Los métodos descritos en este libro pueden emplearse para dibujar estampados de moda con cualquier fin, si bien resultan particularmente idóneos para diseñar prendas de una sola pieza como chales, pareos y bufandas. Cada capítulo incluye varios dibujos que indican dibujar un modelo y irle añadiendo prendas y estampados para crear una ilustración de moda.

Para obtener instrucciones más detalladas acerca de cómo crear ilustraciones de moda y diseñar prendas drapeadas, le recomendamos que consulte otros dos títulos incluidos en esta misma serie de Pepin Press: *Dibujo de figurines para el diseño de moda*, escrito por Elisabetta Drudi y Tiziana Paci, y *Diseño de prendas sin costura*, de Elisabetta Drudi. Ambos libros son un complemento excelente para *Fashion Prints*.

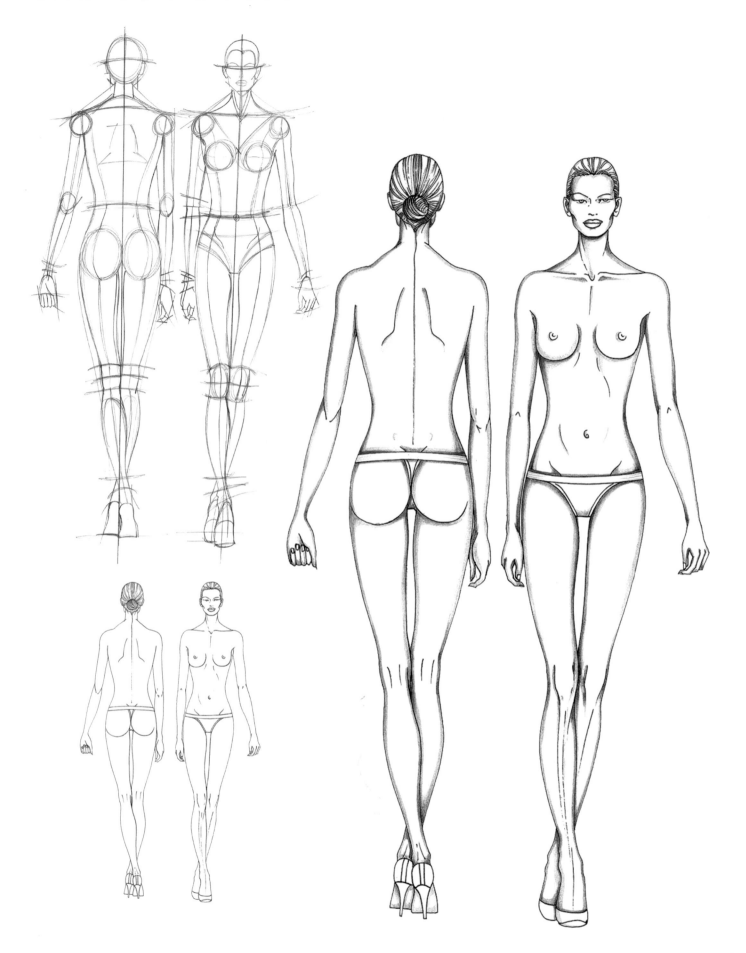

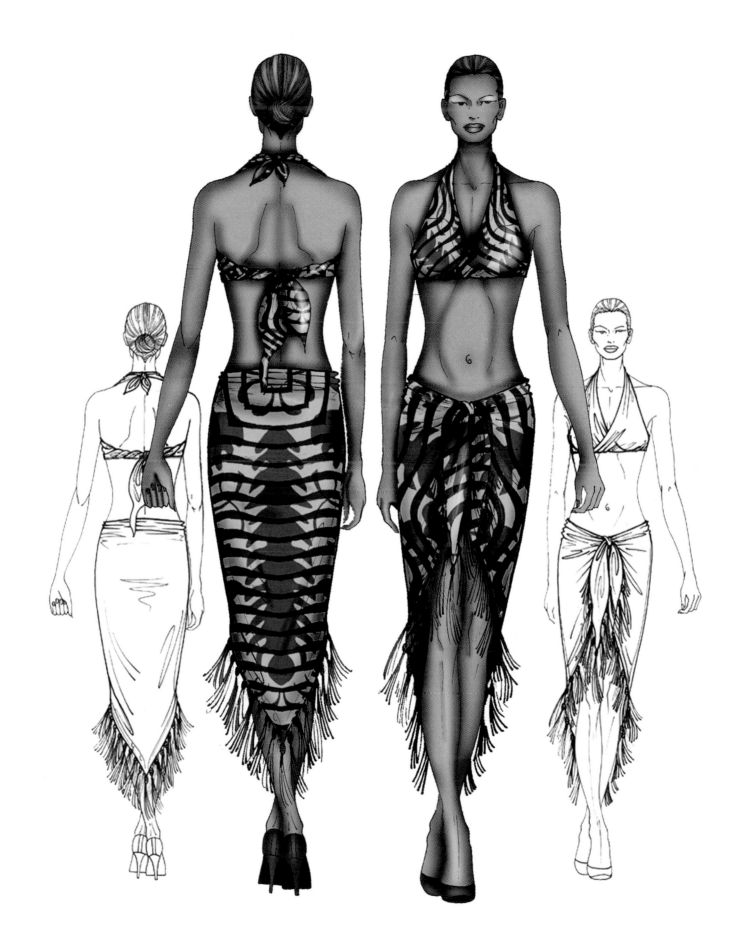

Chapter
Capitolo
Kapitel
Chapitre
Глава
Capítulo

2

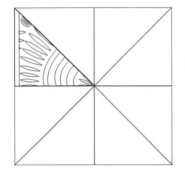 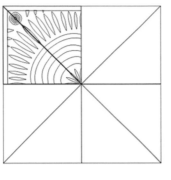 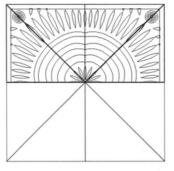 

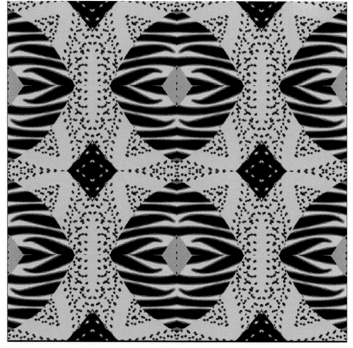

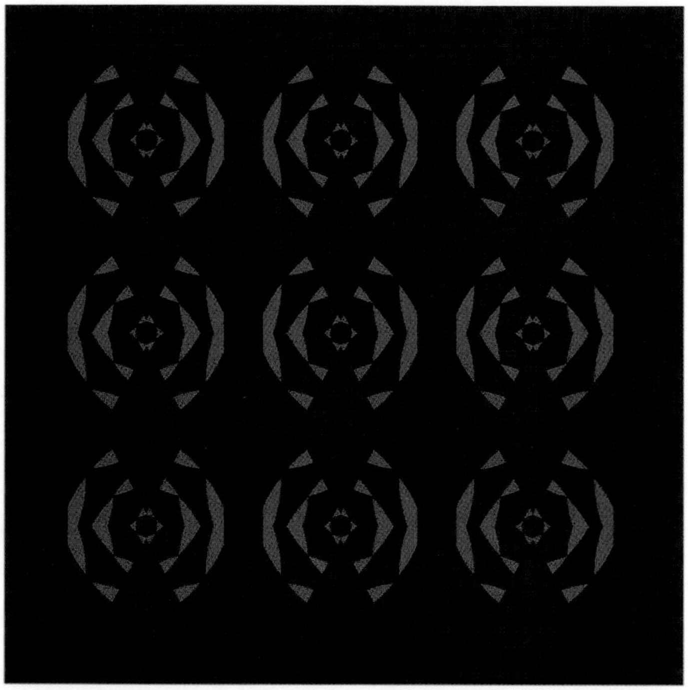

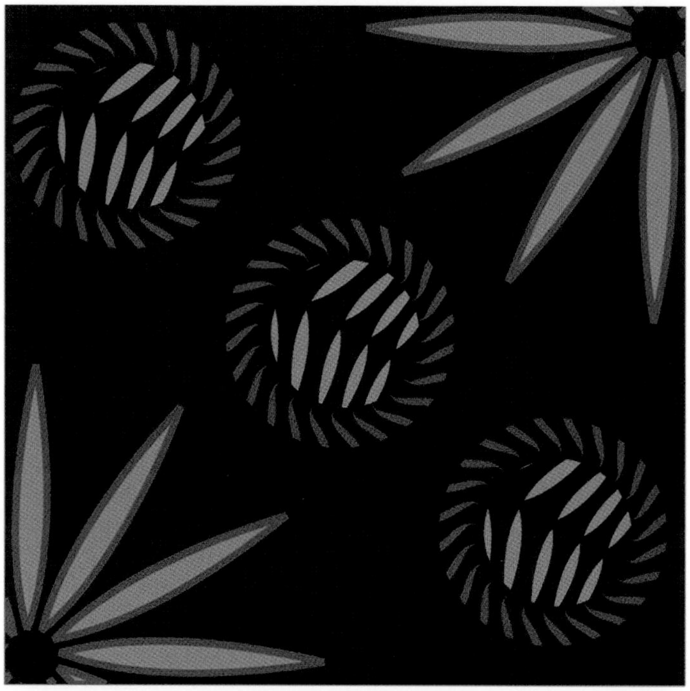

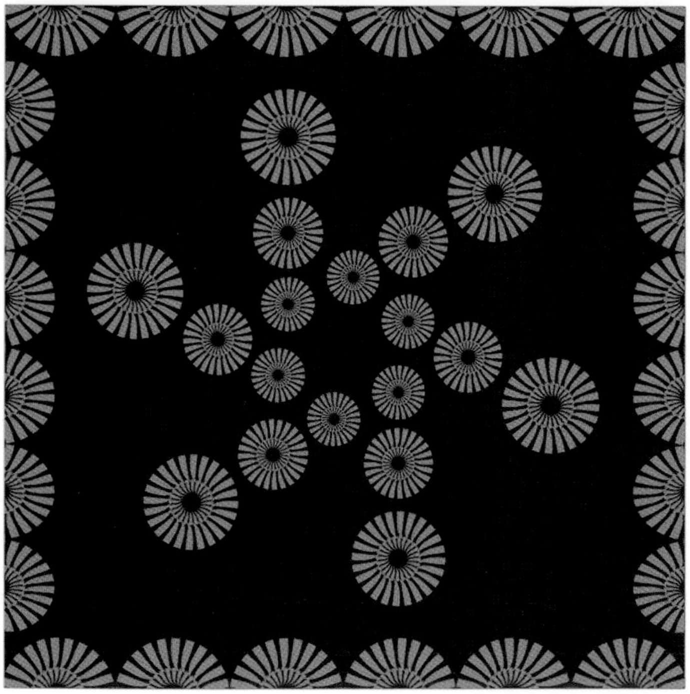

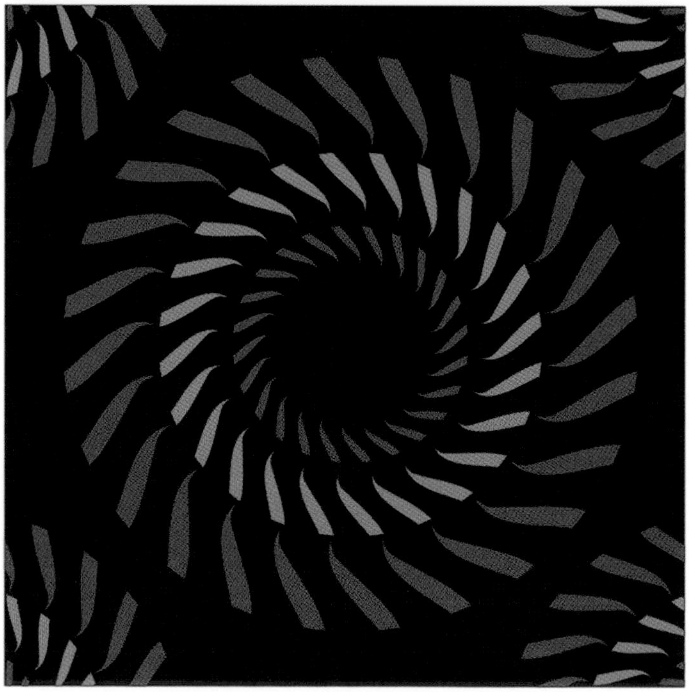

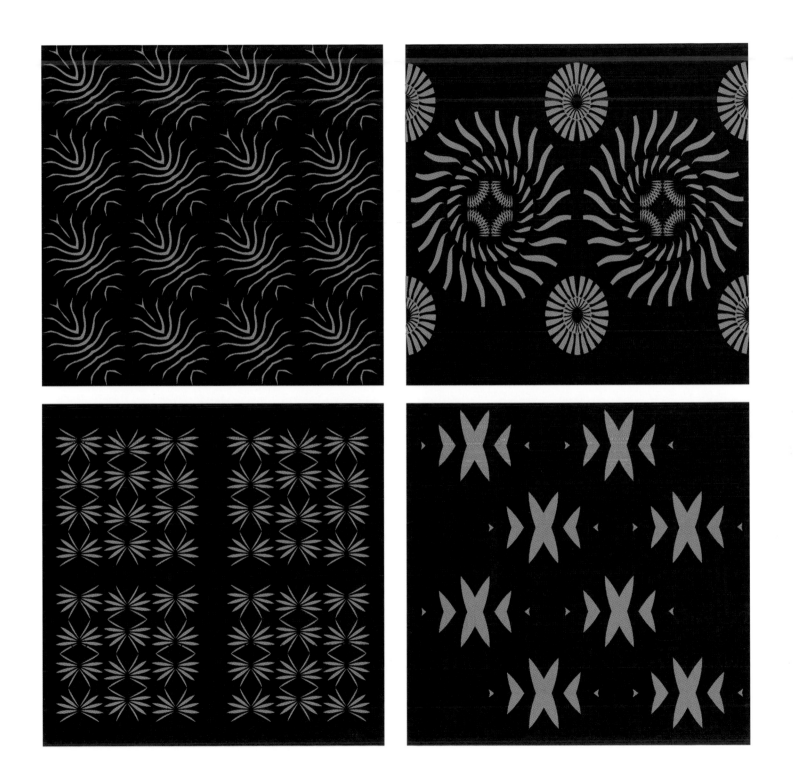

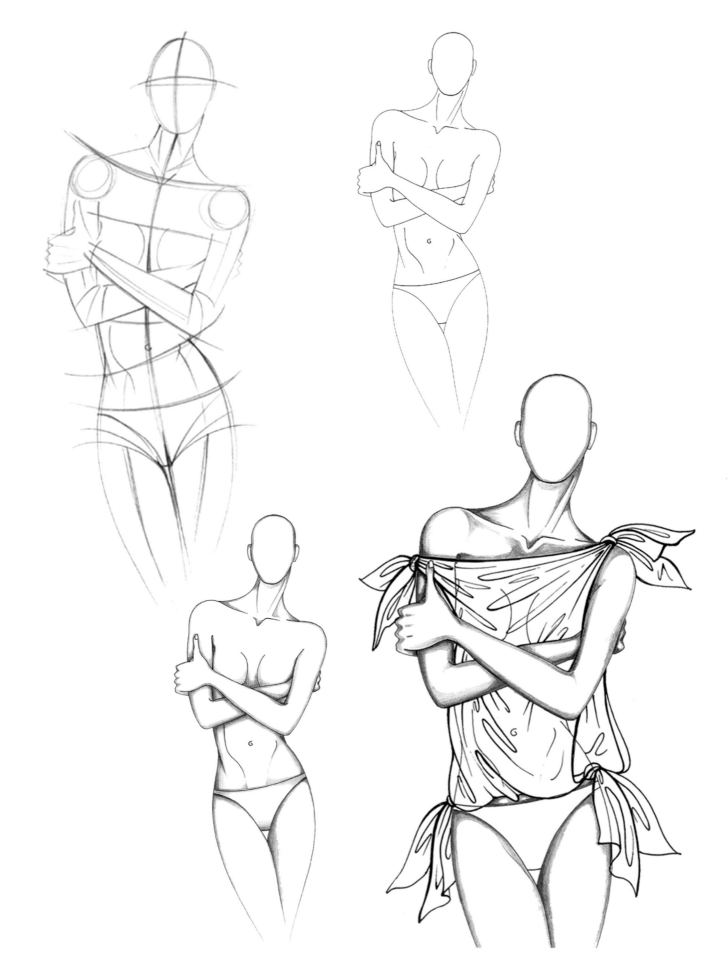

Chapter
Capitolo
Kapitel
Chapitre
Глава
Capítulo

3

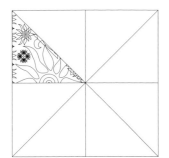 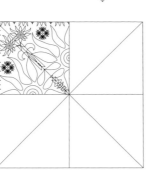  

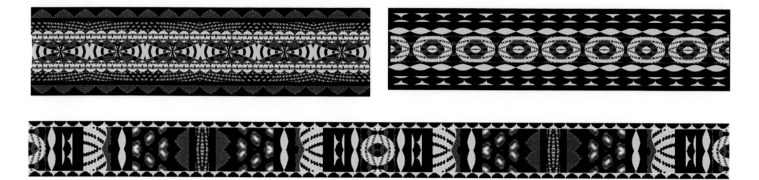

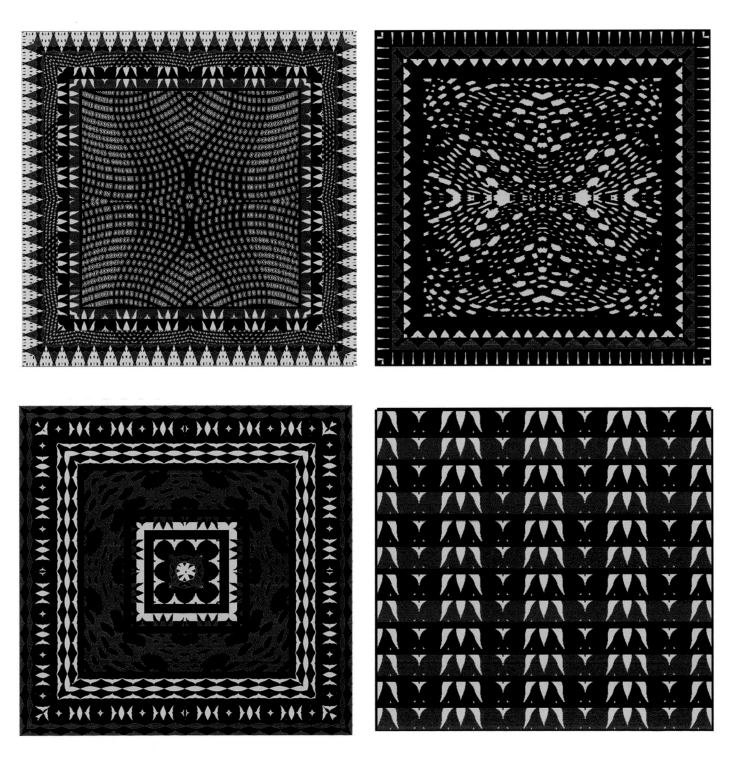

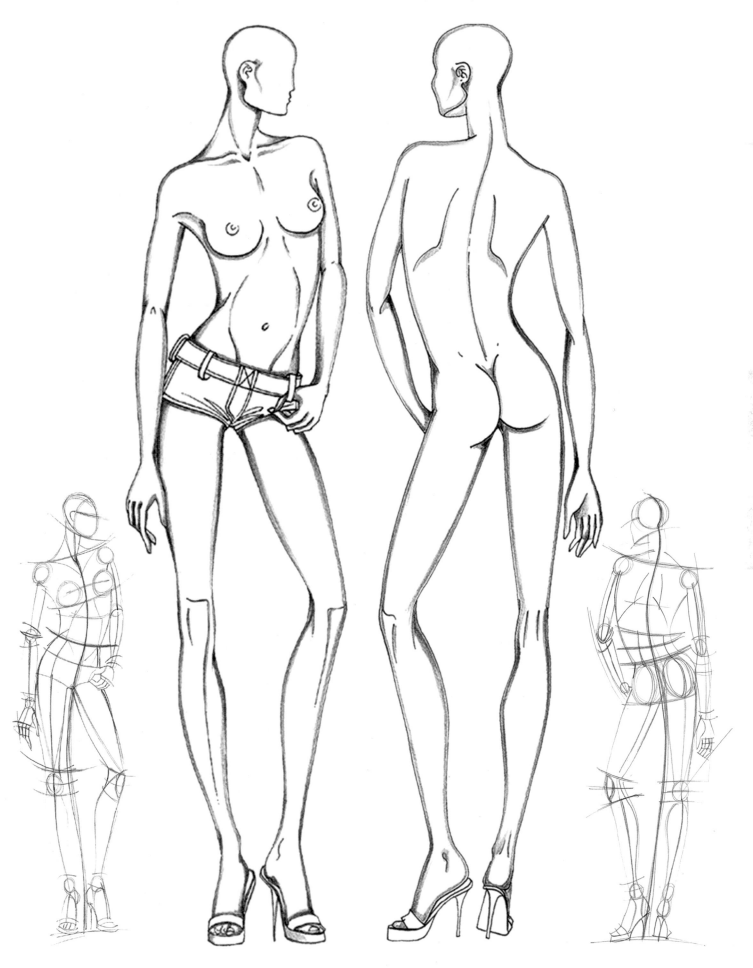

Chapter

Capitolo

Kapitel

Chapitre

Глава

Capítulo

4

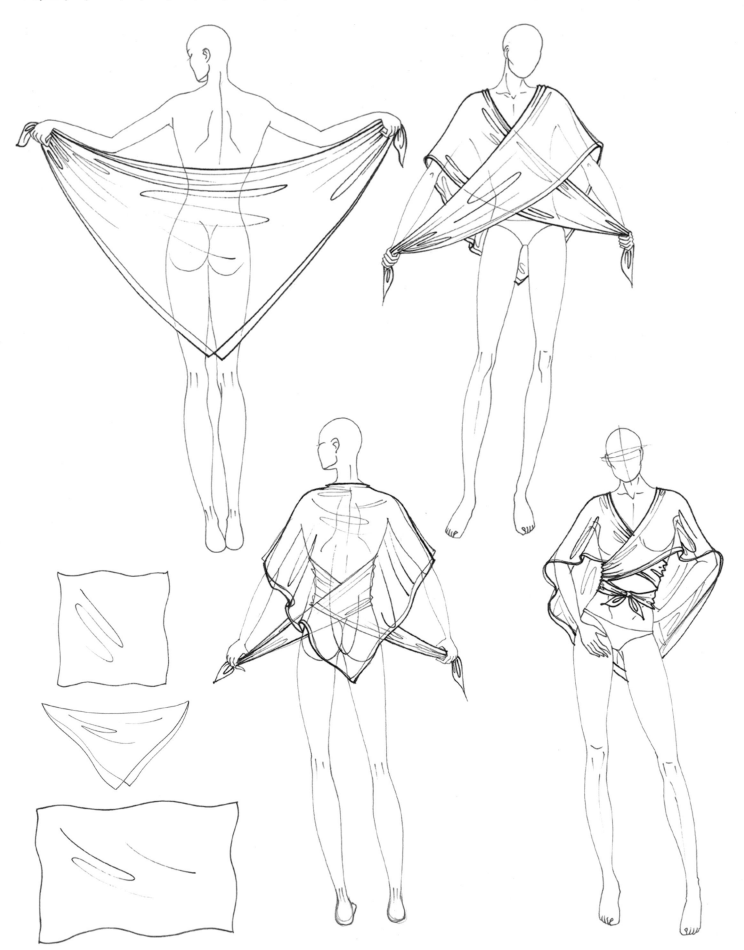

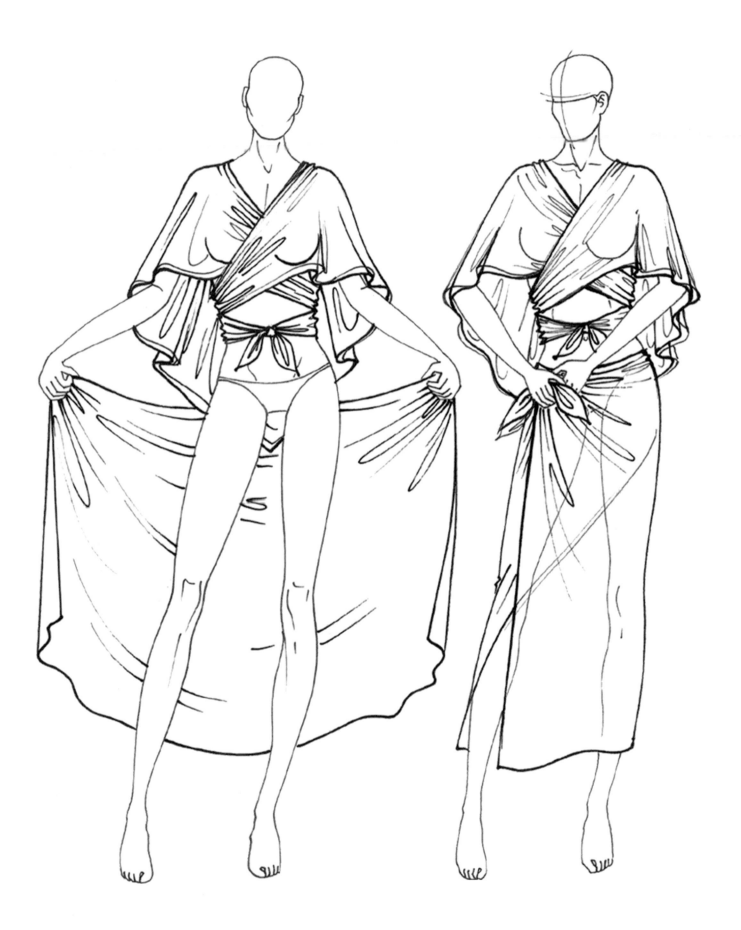

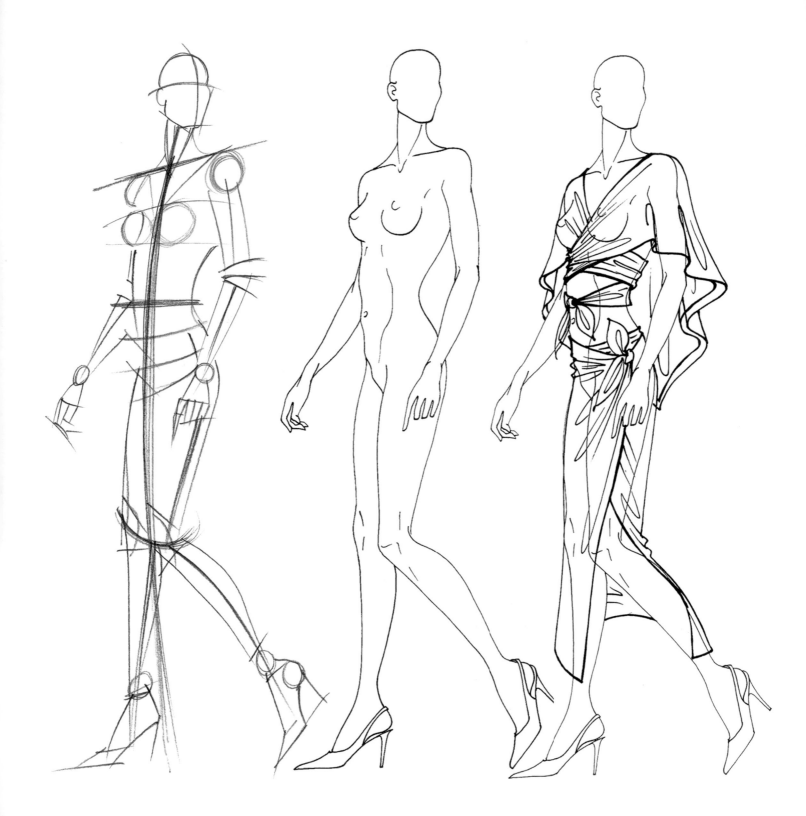

Chapter

Capitolo

Kapitel

Chapitre

Hata

Capítulo

Chapter
Capitolo
Kapitel
Chapitre
Глава
Capítulo

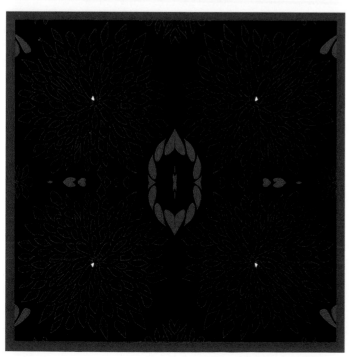

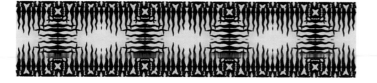

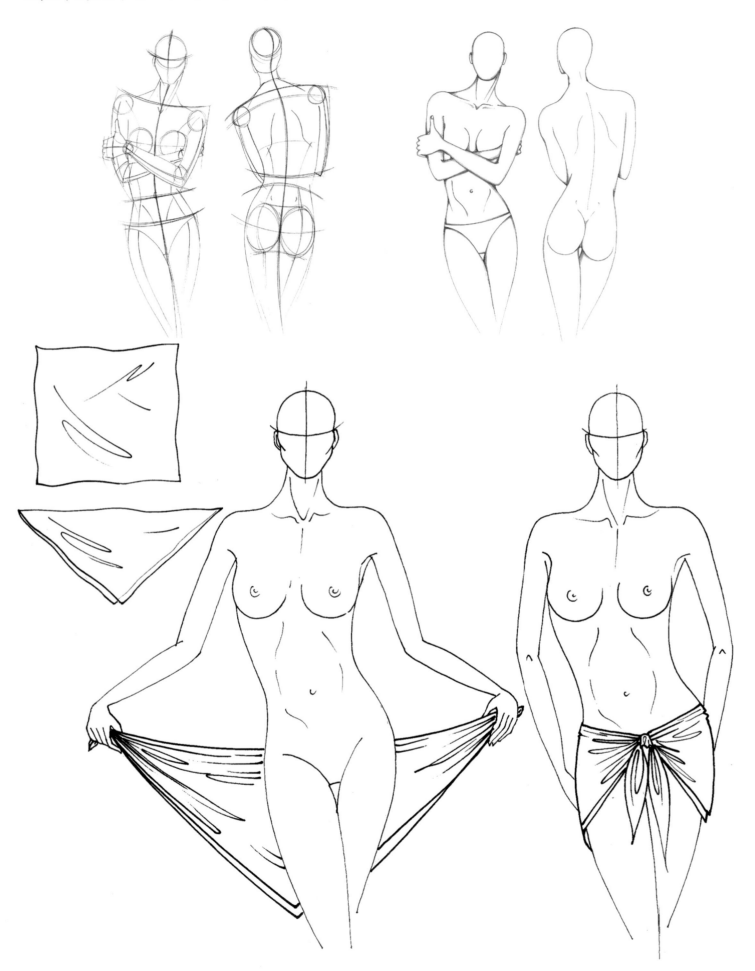

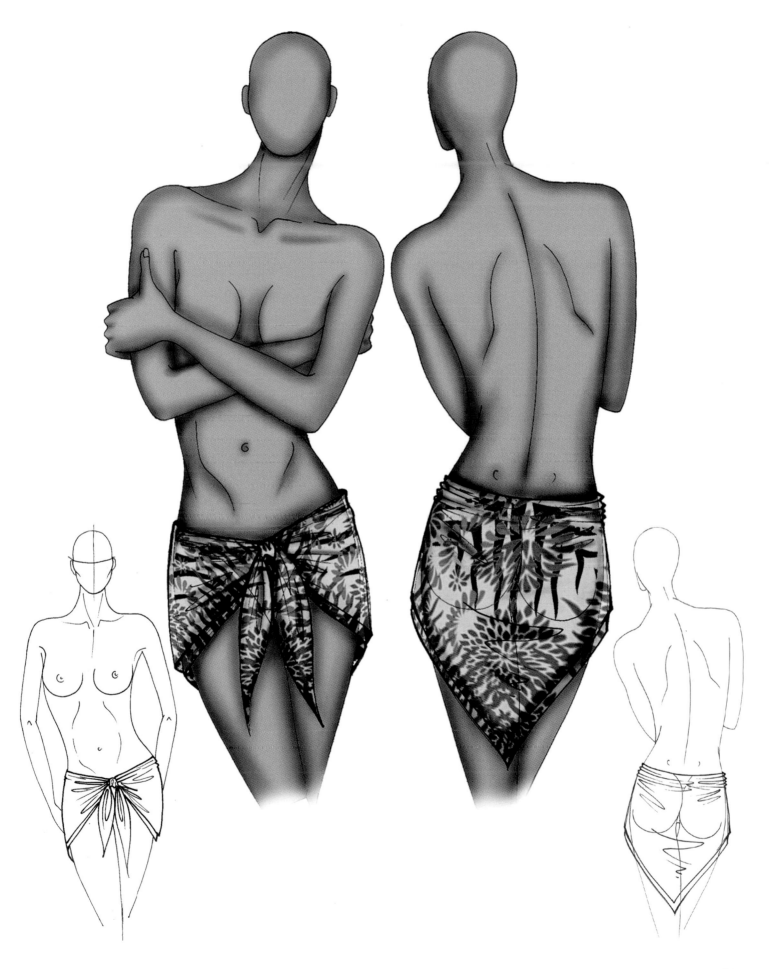

Chapter

Capitolo

Kapitel

chapitre

Глава

Capítulo

Chapter
Capitolo
Kapitel
Chapitre
Глава
Capítulo

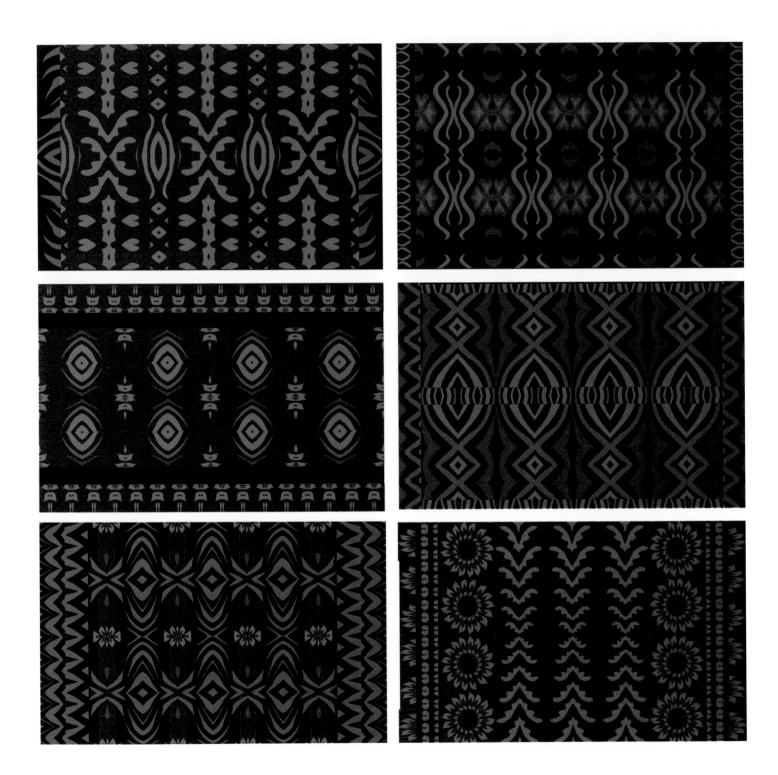

Chapter
Capitolo
Kapitel
Chapitre
Глава
Capítulo

9

Chapter
Capitolo
Kapitel
Chapitre
Глава
Capítulo

10

Chapter

Capitolo

Kapitel

Chapitre

Глава

Capítulo

11

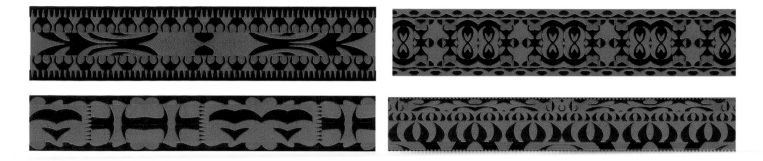

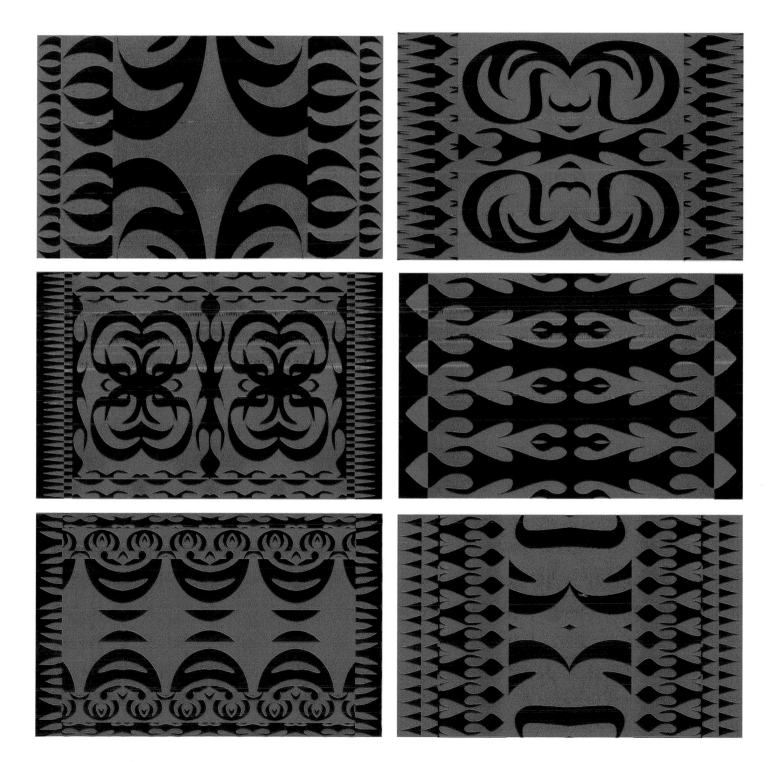

Chapter

Capitolo

Kapitel

Chapitre

Глава

Capítulo

12

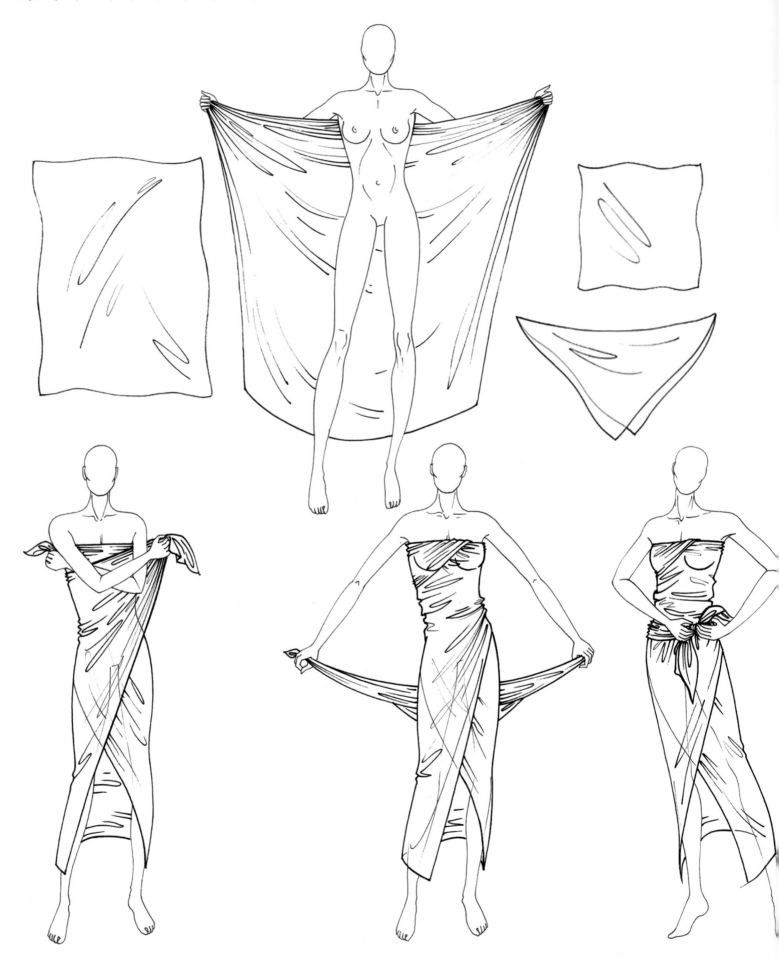